DUCK & GOOSE
COLORING BOOK

Get FREE printable coloring pages and discounted book prices sent straight to your e-mail inbox every week!

Sign up at:

www.adultcoloringworld.net

ISBN-13: 978-1533528643
ISBN-10: 1533528640

PREVIEWS:

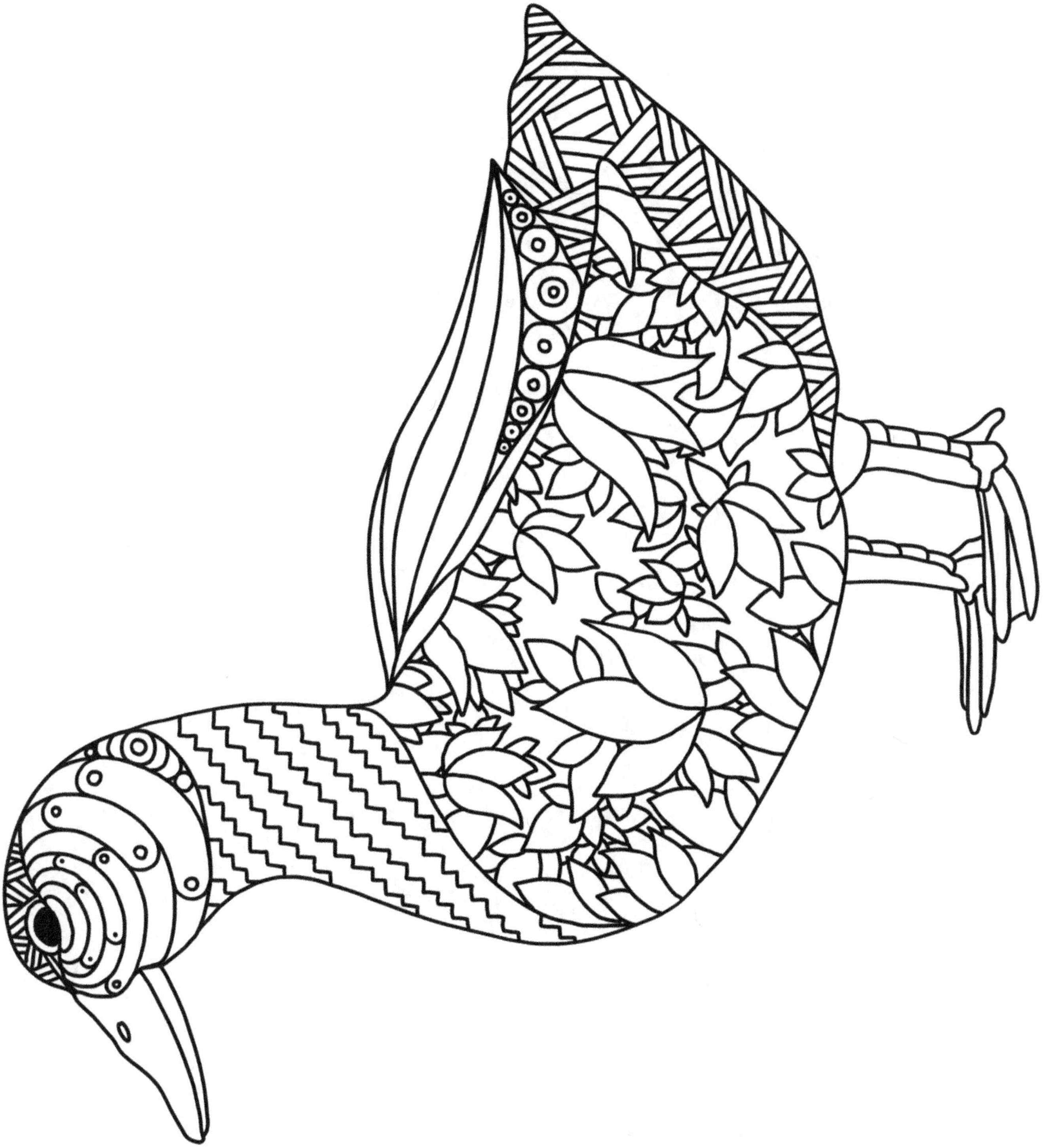

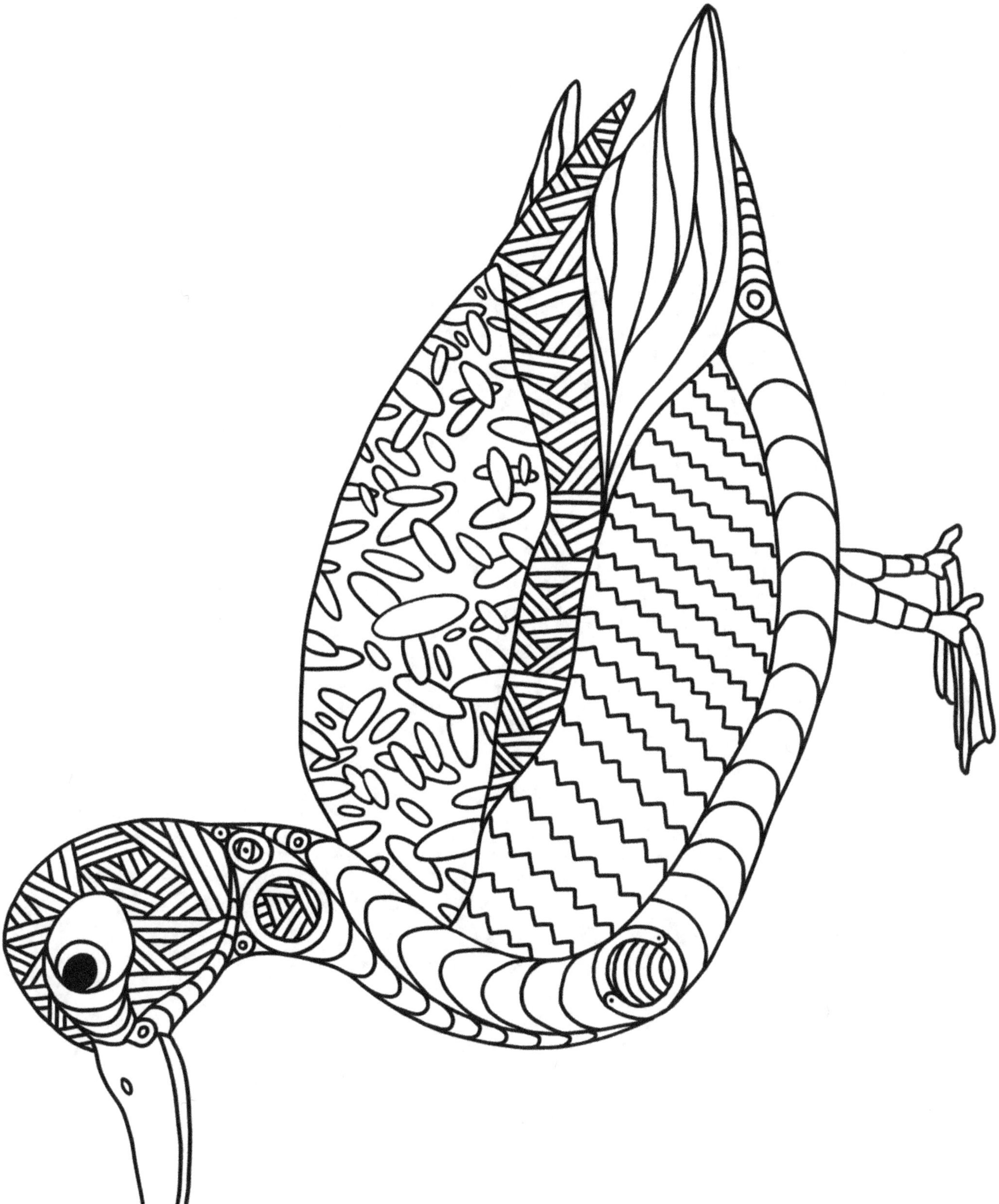

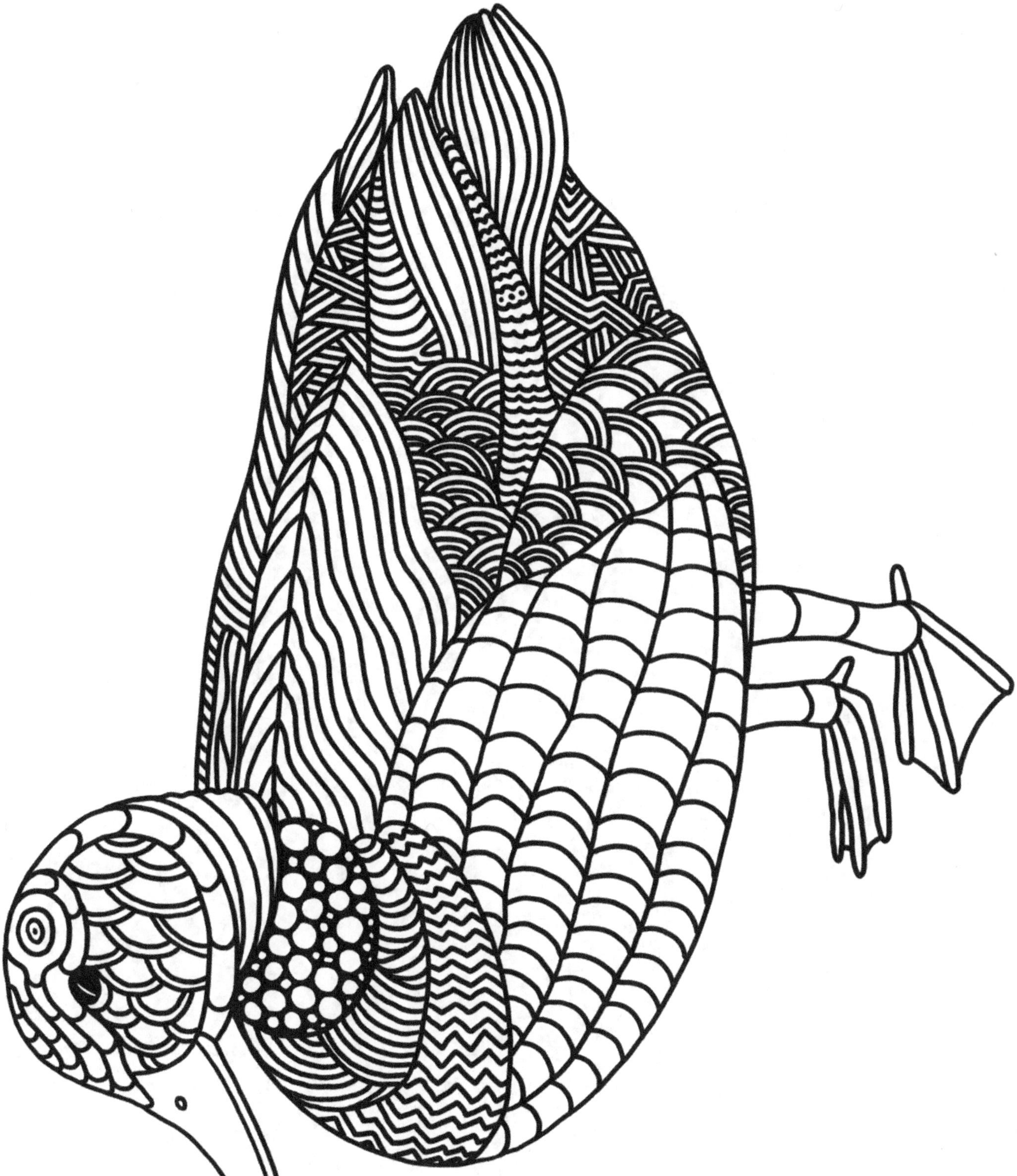

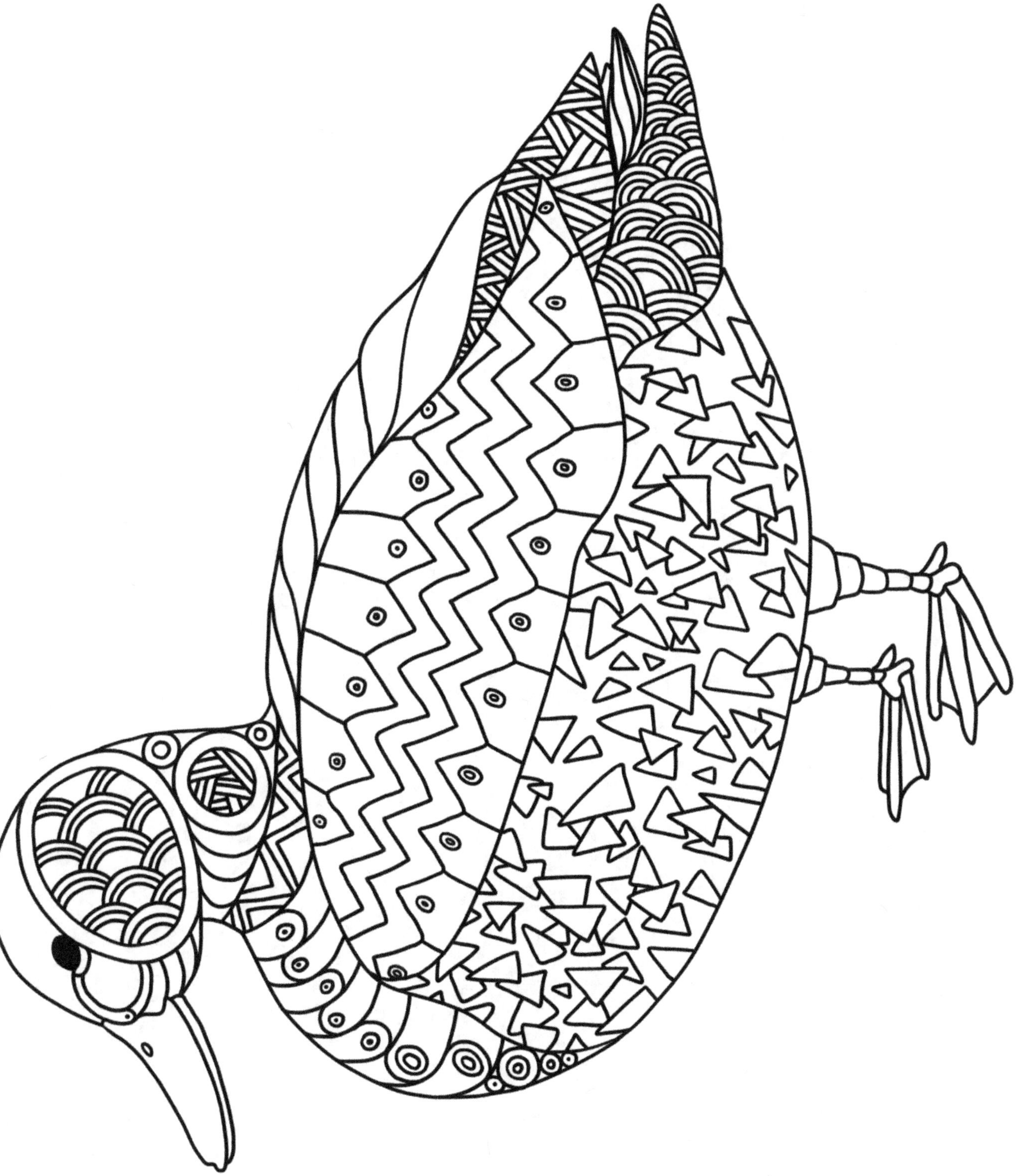

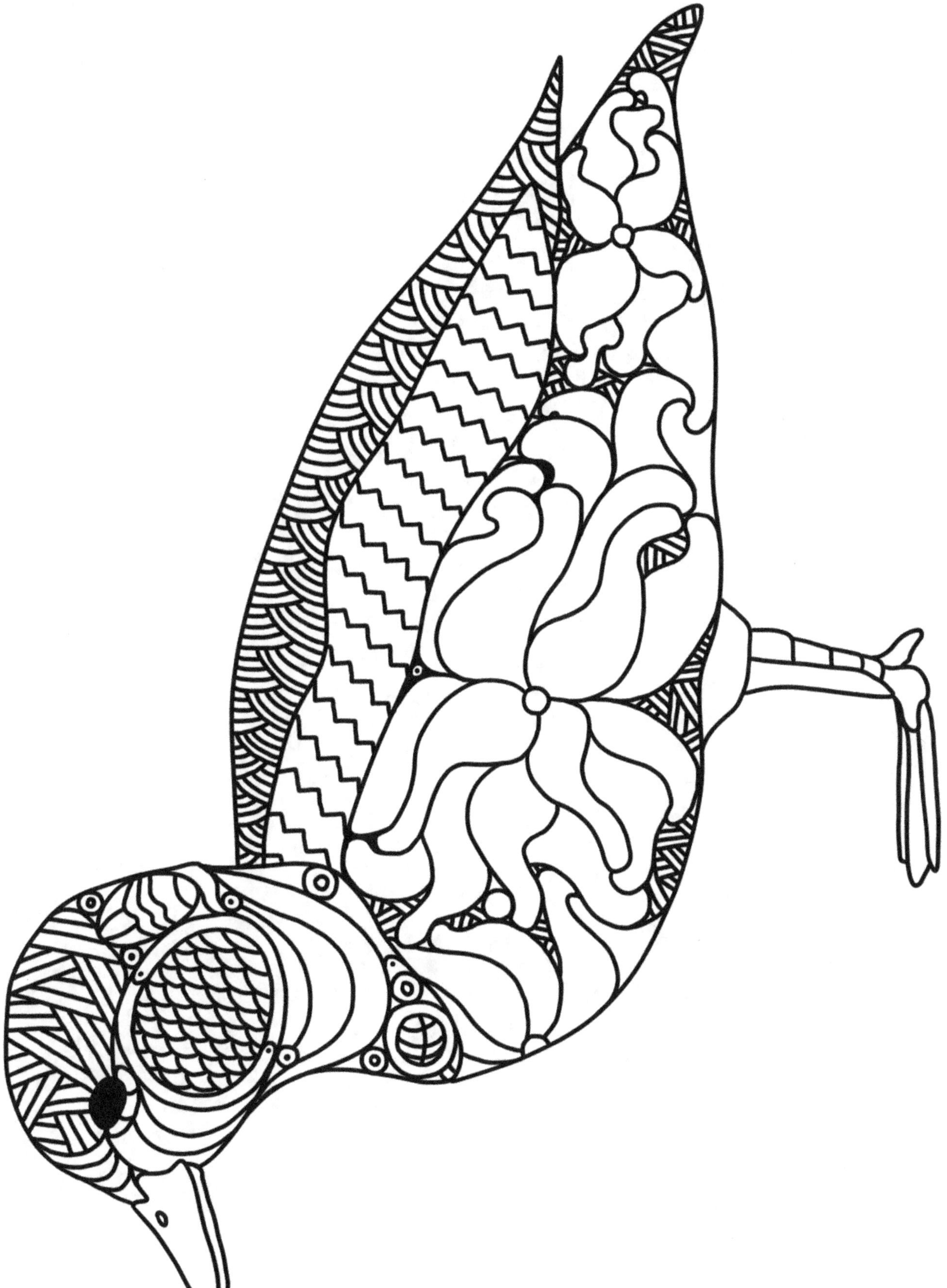

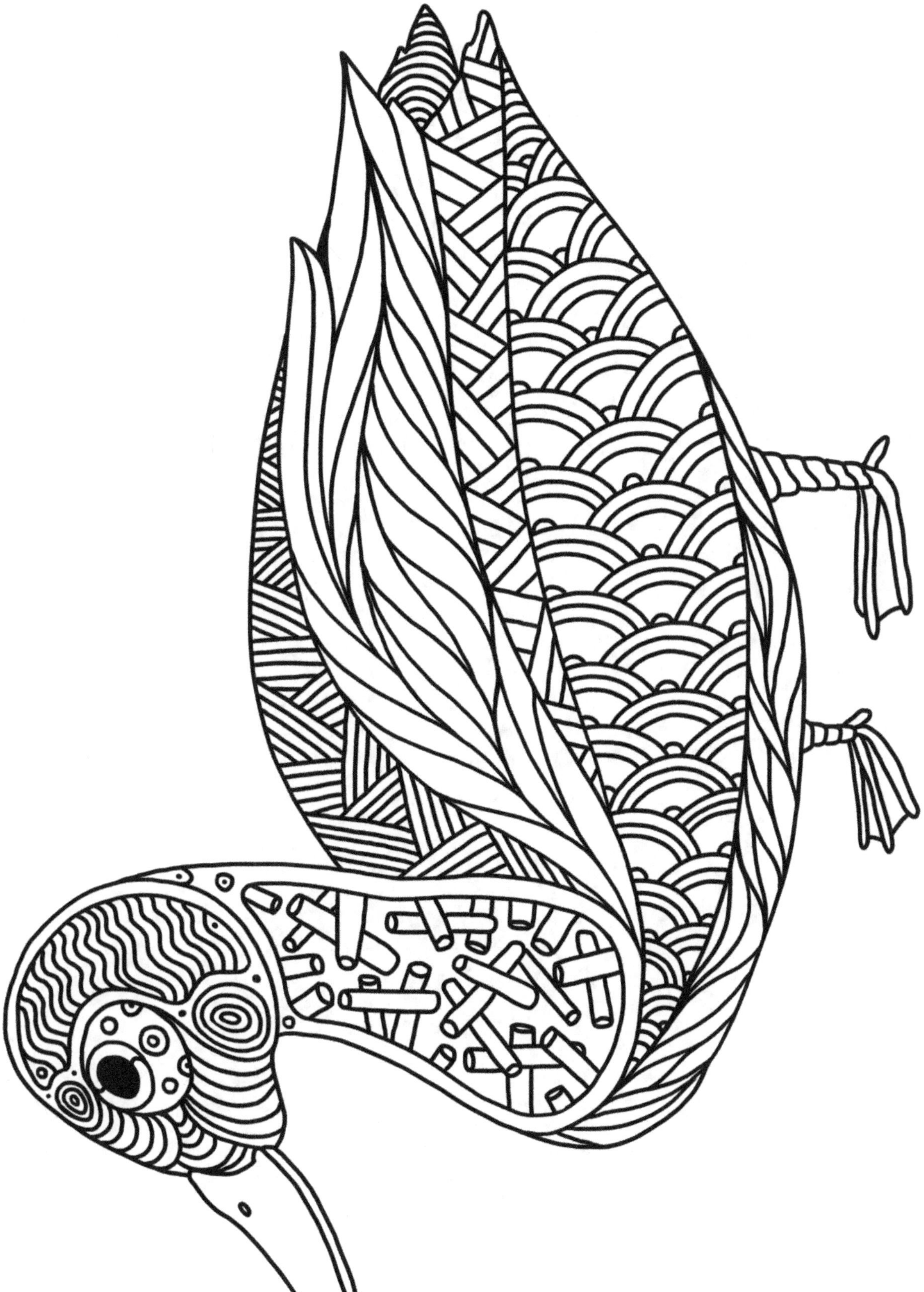

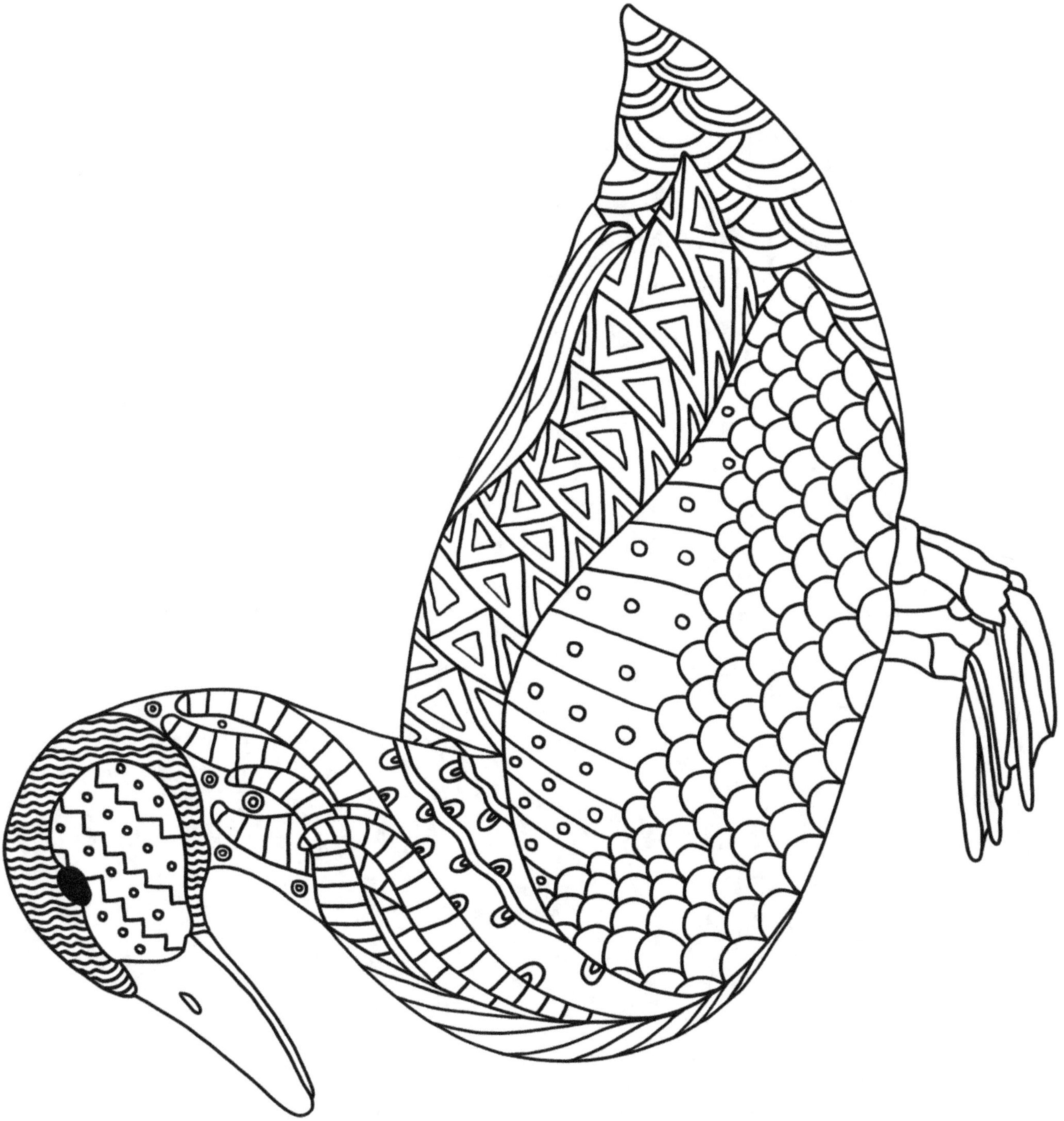

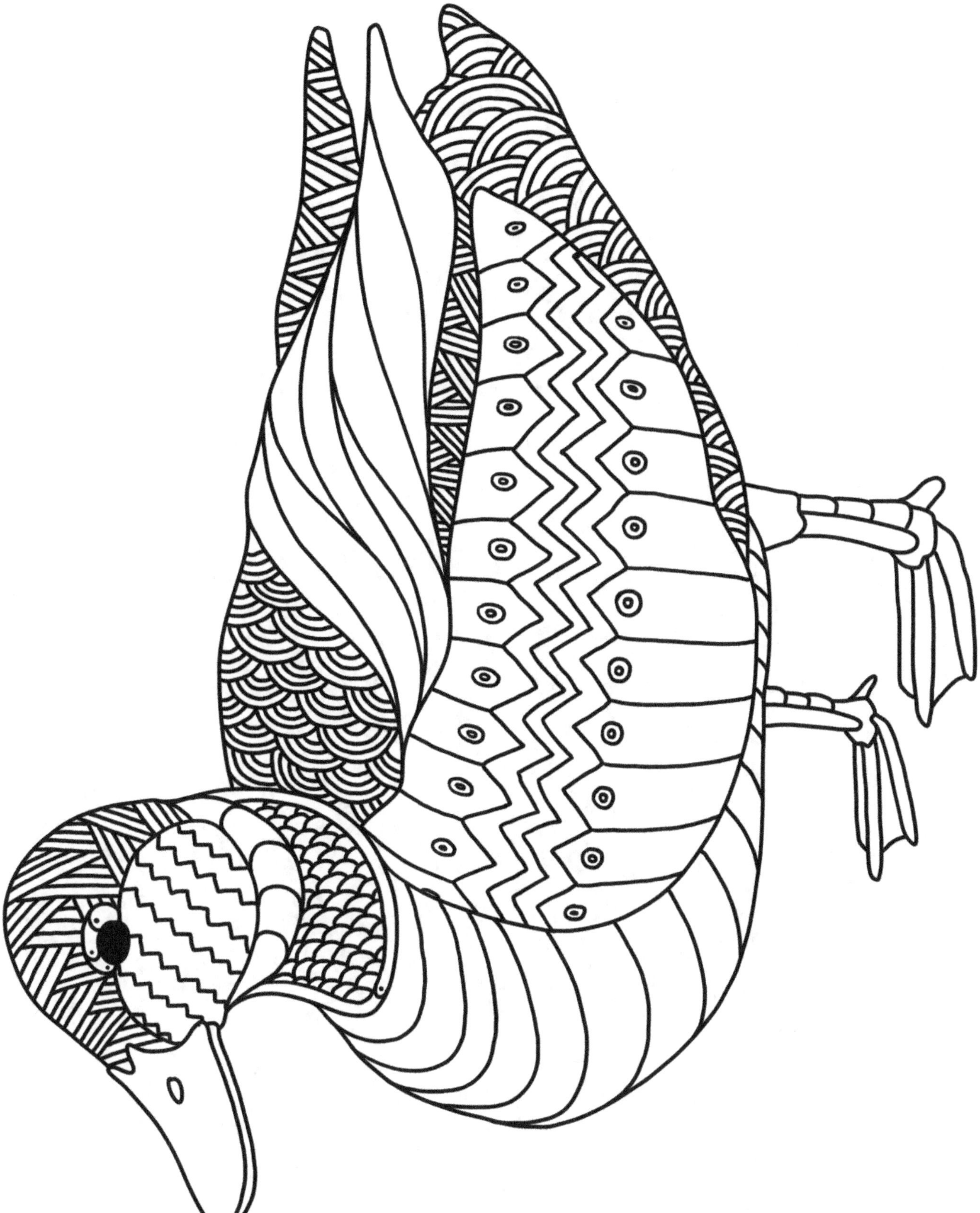

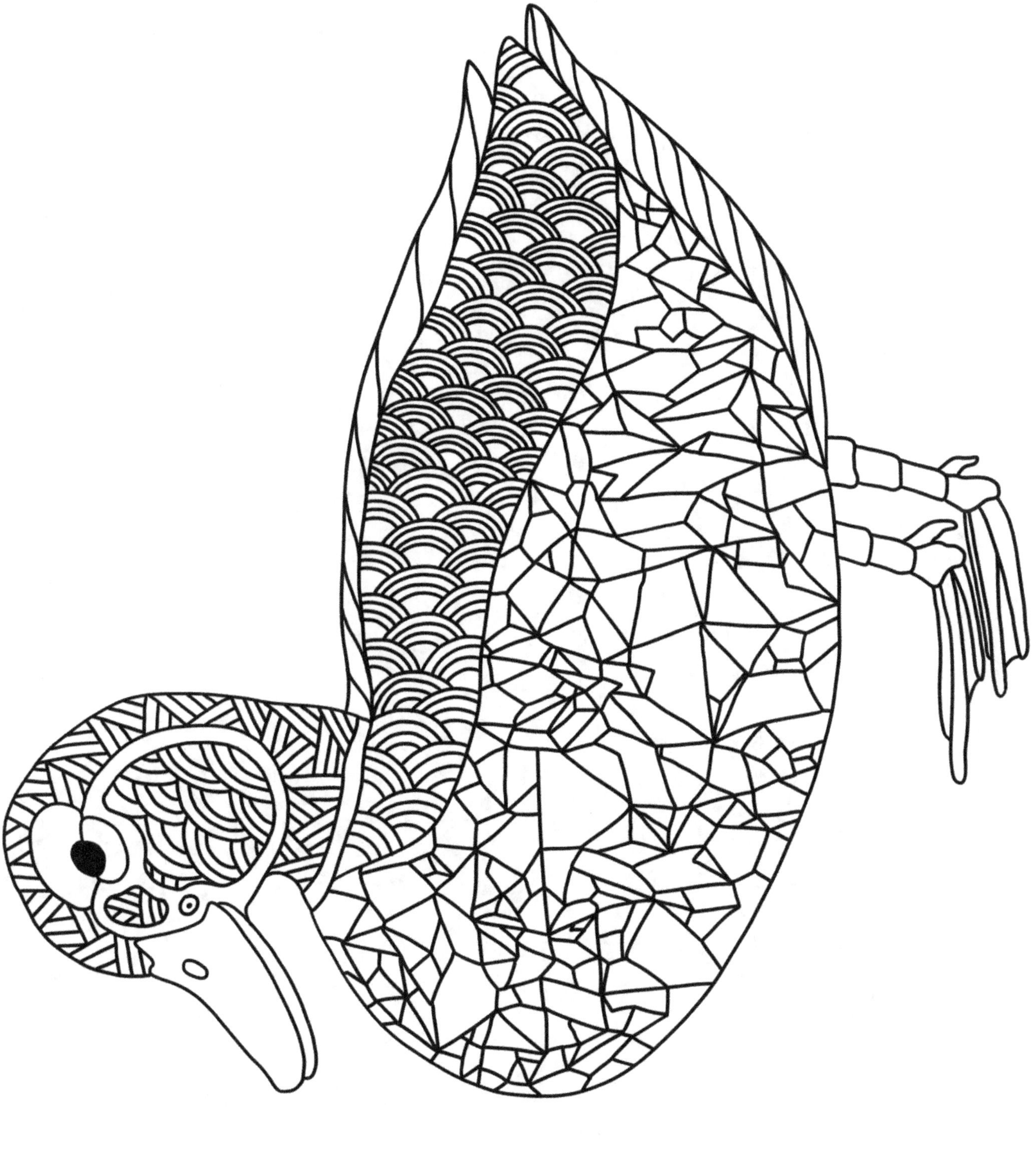

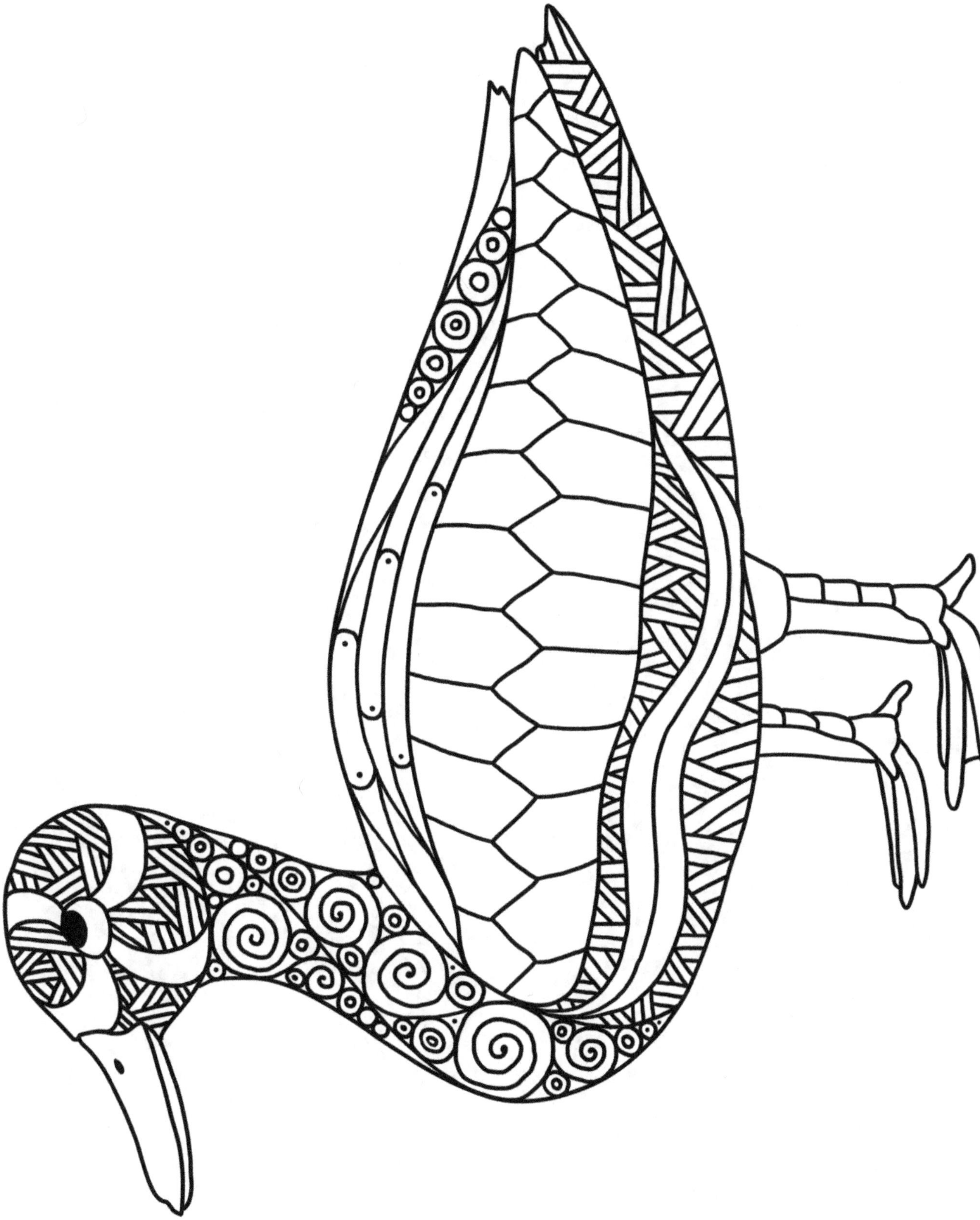

Color Test Page

Color Test Page

www.ingramcontent.com/pod-product-compliance
Lightning Source LLC
Chambersburg PA
CBHW081230280526
45787CB00006B/2594
* 9 7 8 1 5 3 3 5 2 8 6 4 3 *